The Sunken Restaurant

And Other Verse

by Philip Taylor

with drawings by Camilla

The Sunken Restaurant and Other Verse

by Philip Taylor

Drawings by Camilla

Copyright © 2019

ISBN – 9781626131422

Library of Congress Control Number – 2019953518

Published by ATBOSH Media ltd.

Cleveland, Ohio, USA

http://www.atbosh.com

Preface

This collection largely consists of topical pieces written for presentation on television during the period 1982-1984. While many of the news items that stimulated these musings are now forgotten, some of the underlying issues still merit a waspish comment or two. The principal justification for the move from TV to the printed page, though, is that the delightful drawings by my daughter Camilla, then only 11 years old, now replace my soulful face and reproving accents.

One piece in this collection — "Fund Raiser" — differs from the rest in that it isn't attacking anything. It was written as a thank-you to Joan von Herrmann and the production team at station WVIZ. They used it during their membership week, when people are supposed to allow themselves to be overcome with guilt if they don't send in money to support public TV. I've included it here because I was so proud of having found something that rhymed with "laxative".

To my wife, Sarah, whose laughter is always my greatest reward, go my deepest thanks. Without her, I would find it difficult to see the humor hidden in some of the things that happen in this perverse world of ours.

P.T.

Contents

Lions at Large	8
Noah's Ark	10
Payment in Kind	15
Organized Religion	16
The Sunken Restaurant	18
Formula for Success	20
Trouble in Store	22
In Our Right Minds	24
Sperm Wail I	26
Youth to the Fore	28
Sunblind	30
Fund Raiser	33
Environmental Artifacts	36
Sorry — You've Been Troubled	39
Sperm Wail II	41
City Ordnance	44
Stone Deaf	48
Pac-Mate	52
Behind the Highball	54

Bones of Contention	56
Bones of Less Contention 2019	58
Vulnerable	60
Cabbies Curbed	63
Thorns	64
Give Till It Hurts	66
Asking For It	69
Eppur Si Muove — And Yet, It Moves!	70
Teacher's Aid	72
Let Them Eat Cake	74
Free Cheese	76
The Pied Piper of Cleveland	78
About the Author	91

Lions at Large

The Cleveland City Council passed a law to forbid people from having in their homes such animals as lions, bears, and boa constrictors. This prompted protests from some lion owners, who resented such an intrusion on their civil liberties.

If you've got your eye on my big furry lion,
And think that he might be a menace,
You're really quite wrong. Why, I take him along
When I go to the park to play tennis.

The kids love to pet him, and stroke his thick mane;
Then his tail wags as fast as a tail can.
We never get letters that gripe or complain—
At least, not since he ate up the mailman.

We've other fine creatures with all sorts of features;
Our wolverine you'd enjoy stroking.
If our anaconda 'round your neck should wander,
Don't worry, he'll only be choking.

And you'd go bananas to see our piranhas;
Our bathtub won't tempt you to linger.
For though, heaven knows, they've a liking for toes
They do greatly prefer a nice finger.

My lizard's most civilized, although his big swivel eyes
May sometimes suggest indiscreetness.
When it comes to the test, though, the lion's the best;
From that strength comes a wonderful sweetness.

And so I'll defend my fine four-footed friend
In the courts, like a good libertarian.
So don't cast your eye on my harmless poor lion;
He's planning to turn vegetarian.

∽

Noah's Ark

Long years ago God spoke to Noah.
"I begin," He said, "to grow a
Little angry with the world."
He then His awesome plan unfurled.
The earth was with corruption rife,
Reducing God's respect for life.
The world must now be taught a lesson,
So to thoroughly impress on
Men the punishment they'd earned,
All subtle methods would be spurned,
And for chastisement they would get
A large amount of something wet.
Thus Noah had this intimation—
Imminent precipitation!

God said to him "Your good behavior
Warms my heart, so you can save your
Self, your wife, and your three sons,
And their wives too. What must be done's
To build a boat three stories high.
You'll stay comparatively dry
When other men begin to go
Beneath that copious H_2O.
Such safety's not to be despised
When all the world is hydrolyzed."
Noah thought He must be joking.
Build a boat or face a soaking?
God, who isn't known for clowning,
Emphasized that it was drowning
More to which He now inclined.
This concentrated Noah's mind.
Given this exclusive treatment,
Noah made sure that his feet went
Out to where some stately trees
Were swaying gently in the breeze.
Their swaying grew in amplitude
As with his axe he amply hewed
Until they were reduced in number,
Yielding piles of useful lumber.

Quickly then he built his ark,
For now the sky was growing dark
And still they had to take on board
The animals. They'd need inord-
-inate amounts of energy,
Corralling that menagerie,
Assembling bird and beast together,
Ready for a change in weather.

Seven days did they all labor,
Suffering scorn from every neighbor,
None of whom could comprehend
The reason why a man should spend
His time in such an enterprise.
What's more, it was attracting flies,
Two of which old Noah caught
And saved. Although at first he'd thought
That flies he didn't want as boarders,
God had given him his orders—
Two of everything that moved,
Even if it could be proved
That they, unlike the sheep and rabbits,
Had unsanitary habits.

The tasks were finished none too soon,
For now began the great monsoon
That lasted fully forty days,
And drenched the world with such amazing
Force that none survived the morning—
They who lacked God's early warning.
Thus with water all around
The wicked world was duly drowned.
Just Noah's people did God spare;
He let them off with mal de mer.

The sun now shone for all its worth
Upon the saturated earth,
And Noah opened up his ark
To let the creatures disembark.
He thus released his load of fauna,
Urging them to go and spawn a
Generation yet unborn
Of animals that could adorn
Man's table when he needed meat,
Or just as things of beauty greet
Man, when on them he cast his eyes.
He also then released the flies.

Then in the sky God cast a rainbow,
Promising he'd ne'er again po-
-llute the earth with waters deep.
This was a covenant he'd keep:
That rainbow standing there would say
That He'd not choose that self-same way
To punish man if once more he
Should start to act most sinfully.

Now, when a contract comes from God
It must be thought a little odd
To scrutinize the bottom line
To see if in that print so fine
There might not be some little clause
That maybe for sufficient cause
Could then a punishment permit
That differed just a little bit
From that experienced before.

But don't you think that you'd be sore,
And would it not arouse your ire,
If you were God, and from your higher
Vantage point could see man strive
At nothing that would help him thrive,
But rather working harder still
To build atomic overkill
By adding to the nuclear stockpile,
Making bombs around the clock while
Others work on neutron beams
Most capable, or so it seems,
Of killing indiscriminately?
Is it time to build an ark?
I haven't seen a rainbow lately,
And the sky is growing dark.

Payment in Kind

In 1983 President Reagan announced a program in which farmers would receive shipments of surplus grain in return for not planting crops. In other words, they would be paid for not growing grain by being sent some of the grain they were not growing.

Spare a thought for the farmer who toils in the fields
And produces the food for our table.
His crops give increasingly generous yields
As he works just as hard as he's able.

The grain he produces he sells to the Feds,
Who then export it out to the Russians.
We really can't stand seeing underfed Reds,
Though that still is a point of discussion.

But now there's a plan that will turn things around
And will spare every farmer much botherment;
In future he won't grow a thing on his ground,
But will gets lots of grain from the government.

This clever idea may soon rapidly spread
With a speed that could be record-breaking;
And then we can all spend a fortnight in bed,
While the Feds send us what we're not making.

You know how it feels to make automobiles
And to meet productivity quotas.
Now workers at Ford can just play shuffleboard
While the government sends them Toyotas.

I spoke to a man who's employed at a stable—
He gathers and sells horse manure.
I asked if he thought that he'd ever be able
To see this idea's great allure.

Would he like to see his work put in reverse?
Did the prospect arouse any fears?
His answer was brief, to the point, and quite terse—
"They've been sending us that stuff for years!"

Organized Religion

The Roman Catholic Diocese of Phoenix refused to marry a couple because the man was a quadriplegic, and unable to consummate the union.

A man in a wheelchair has promised that he'll share
His life with the girl he will wed.
And she, in her turn, will all other men spurn
From now till the day they are dead.

They wanted my blessing, so it was distressing
That I could not share their elation.
But that sort of marriage the Church will discourage
That does not allow consummation.

If you are disabled, alas, you are labeled
As one whose engagement must falter.
If you're quadriplegic to us you're a reject;
We won't let you wheel to the altar.

Your thoughts about marriage I will not disparage,
Though on them you should place some checks.
We know that there's caring, and loving and sharing,
But much more important is sex.

If for marriage inclined, then a woman should find
Someone whole, not a physical mess.
And then, I must stress, send him here to confess,
And to tell me about his prowess.

Though this ruling diocesan makes you feel cross it's an
Edict from our Papal College
That all married women will only please Him in this
World if they have carnal knowledge.

The Sunken Restaurant

A Cleveland restaurant owner had bought a 210-foot excursion boat which he was planning to convert into a floating restaurant. Unfortunately, it broke loose from its moorings and sank in the Cuyahoga river.

It would have been nice to have dinner afloat
With champagne, and pâté of goose liver.
But now all that's left is a wet *table d'hôte,*
For the boat has sunk under the river.

Gourmets won't flock for a night on the town
To that mooring so damp and so foggy.
You can't serve good food on a boat that's gone down;
The french fries get terribly soggy.

To choose between restaurants sometimes one's urged,
And the merits of each are debated.
Remember, one lies 'neath the river submerged,
With its meat fully submarinated.

Six feet under water you can't toss a pancake;
The management shouldn't be blamed.
And it is such a pity that beefsteak Diane
At the tableside cannot be flamed.

If you get an itch for a French-dip sandwich
Then you're sunk if that boat has been junked.
It really is no use, to ask for the *au jus*
When everything's been fully dunked.

So when in July we go down to the lake
For refreshment, there won't be a boat.
We can order a Pepsi, a Coke or a shake,
What a shame we can't order afloat.

∞

Formula for Success

One controversial question involves the sale of infant formula in less-developed countries. Is it morally wrong for a big multinational corporation to promote powdered milk as an alternative to breast feeding in a country where there is no supply of clean water, or should it be thought of just as a case where the buyer must beware? This was a current issue in 1982, and is sadly still unresolved.

Part I

In the jungle, damp and hot,
A mother feeds her little tot.
She holds him to her welcome breast
Then lays him on the ground to rest.
She stays alert, for in these parts
Some dangers lurk — not poisoned darts
Nor tigers fierce, not snakes that kill,
But something that's more serious still—
A danger of another ilk—
The man who sells the powdered milk!

But here he comes, in coat so white;
Advice he gives just must be right.
His scornful look now seems to say
"You're not still feeding that old way!
Here, buy a little can or two
And use it. See what it will do!
Just mix it up with two parts water;
Give it to your little daughter."
Hearing such assuring tones
She gives him all the cash she owns.
But after this auspicious start
Disaster strikes.

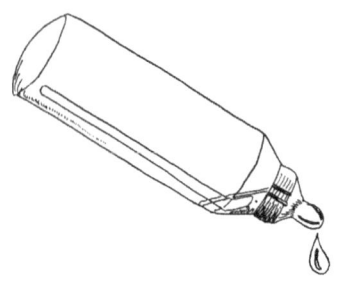

Four things depart:
The first to go — the salesman;
Next week the contents of the can
Are spent; and now she surely knows
That her own milk no longer flows;
The fourth departure drives her wild—
She loses then her little child.
The mother grieves, the baby dies,
But someone's profits start to rise.

Part II

We move on to another place
Where formula now sells apace.
A third-world urban slum, we find,
Can be a stage for that nice kind
White-coated lady with the spiel
That says milk powders cure and heal.
She's dressed to look just like a nurse
And so for better or for worse
The local mothers heed her voice
And infant formula's their choice.

One hurries home with can in hand,
And, though she doesn't understand
Directions printed on the label,
Tries as hard as she is able.
Water here cannot be trusted,
Coming through a tap that's rusted,
From a source that's most impure
With leakage from a broken sewer.
Her only bottle's none too clean—
It's inside looks distinctly green—
But she won't let her baby stop
Till he has finished every drop.
That "nurse" had said in glowing tones
That powdered milk makes healthy bones.
Imagine her hysteria
When coliform bacteria
And other germs in ample ration
Kill her son by dehydration.

> Way off in another land
> The chairman of the board will stand
> And to a hushed, expectant room
> Describe how sales begin to boom
> And stockholders will clap at all
> That good return on capital.

∞

Trouble in Store

A businessman had bought an old-established chain of department stores, and had made known ambitious plans for their operation. However, as soon as Christmas was over he announced that they would close.

Most of our stores we've decided to close;
They just were not making a profit.
My heart was quite set on some fine stores like those,
But now it's gone totally off it.

We'd said they'd stay open, but now they must go—
Please don't think I was being deceiving.
We gave them a fortnight to see what they'd do;
Now its severance pay they're receiving.

With those stores losing money, they just had to cease;
The balance sheet speaks with great clarity.
So we fire employees quick as chickens can sneeze—
We're a business, you know, not a charity.

Sales of pianos were sounding quite flat;
There was sag both in sweaters and stockings.
In beds nothing happened — 'nough said about that—
And electrical goods were just shocking.

Mr. Jones had sold carpets for thirty-one years;
Miss Kowalski sold dresses and such.
So we said, as we threw them right out on their ears,
"For those years, thank you **so** very much!"

You see they don't realize, those people who shout
In tones full of anger and hate,
That it isn't just stores that we're talking about,
But lucrative real estate.

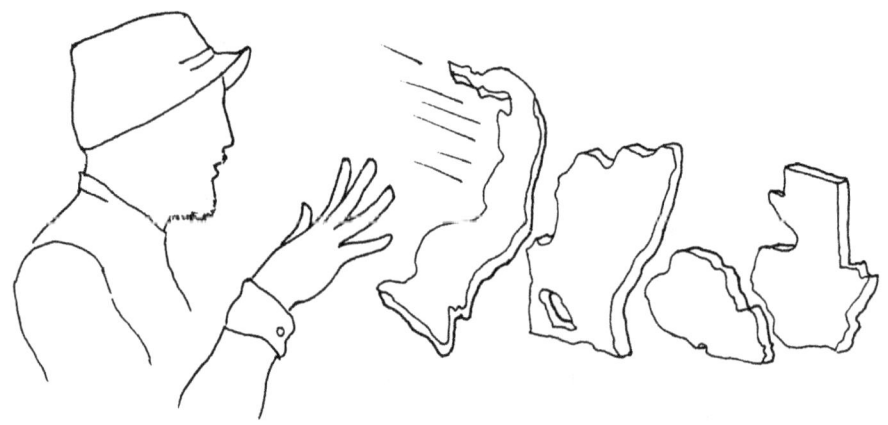

In Our Right Minds

The armed forces of the junta government of El Salvador were responsible for tens of thousands of civilian deaths during the period 1980–1990. The US provided millions of dollars per day in military aid.

The nightly news shown on TV
Increasingly now seems to be
Replete with stories of the war
That's growing in El Salvador.
The government there daily pleads;
More tanks and guns are urgent needs.
On this America's divided;
Is the issue so one-sided?
And is José Napoleón
Duarte's war a holy one?

Some think the problem is not new
And get a sense of *déjà vu*,
Remembering when Uncle Sam
First sent advisors to Vietnam—
"The light is there at tunnel's end
If only we more arms would send."
Our leader we hear from. He knows
That states can fall like dominoes.
And if your strength should start to flag you are
Facing a new Nicaragua.
When fighting leftist insurrection
Two howitzers beat one election.

So it seems that we may opt to
Send a hundred helicopters
Down to join the firefight
'Cos we don't think the left is right,
And we will see that land in flames
Before the left can stake their claims.
Or are we of all sense bereft
To think it's right when nothing's left?

∞

$$\delta F = \int \{a\Delta^2 + b\Delta^4 + c|\nabla\Delta|^2\}\vec{dr} \quad !$$

Sperm Wail I

An institution called the "Repository for Germinal Choice" had been set up in Escondido, California. Its plan was to make available the genetic material of Nobel-Prize-winning scientists to women who wanted to have "creative, intelligent children".

A gentleman in Escondido
Told the world last year that he'd
Originate a simple scheme
To further every mother's dream
Of giving birth to brilliant offspring.
His idea, though many scoff, brings
Help from men with Nobel prizes—
Yes, that's what he advertises—
To the aid of any lady
With a husband who's afraid he
Might be judged as rather stupid.
She'll reject the darts of Cupid,
Subjugating her libido
With a trip to Escondido,
And, in clinical seclusion
Take a seminal infusion,
Hoping, when the deed is done,
That she'll produce a brainy son.

This raised objections from the Church
Who questioned the genetic search,
And said it was adultery.
Some saw in its result a real
Problem then to name the daddy
Of this intellectual laddie.
Was it, asks one worldly cynic,
Husband, scientist, or clinic?

I would ask of this endeavor
Whether people who are clever
Are the world's most pressing need,
And, if we must go gathering seed,
Should not we rather try to find
More people who are good and kind?

Youth to the Fore

The government proposed to relax many of the federal regulations restricting the use of child labor. Younger children would then be allowed to work for longer hours in a wider variety of jobs.

To the guy pumping gasoline I said, would it hassle him
To change my old windshield wiper?
Sure! That he would do in a minute or two,
If in turn I would first change his diaper.

Early this summer I needed a plumber
To fix up a leaky old tap.
When I phoned him, his office said "Pay him in toffees,
And he'll come right after his nap."

With a pain in my toe, to a doctor I'd go,
On whose tender years I will not dwell.
He'd say "Off with your clothes from your toes to your nose,
For I really do love 'show and tell'."

A youthful stonemason sat down with a basin
Of soup, which he noisily slurped.
"Today," said his neighbor "he'll do no more labor
Until he's been thoroughly burped."

Some unemployed men watched a young boy of ten
Digging ditches with all of his power.
He said "Wielding this tool is more tiring than school,
But they pay me a dollar an hour!

"Though I never will shirk from this backbreaking work
I do envy my Dad in this heat.
Now he has been fired just so I could be hired—
He's at home watching Sesame Street."

∞

Sunblind

In 1983 the Nuclear Regulatory Commission — the NRC — announced its new goals for the safety of nuclear reactors. This was prompted by the meltdown of a reactor at Three Mile Island in Pennsylvania in 1979. Among the alternative ways of generating electricity at that time, solar cells were little used in the US, and their production was largely confined to Japanese companies.

The NRC's new safety goals,
Which really should be highly rated,
Say that thirteen thousand souls
Could be from bodies separated,
Some day in the future, when
A big reactor blows its top.
It makes you almost ask if then
Reactor building ought to stop.

They've thought of a nice name for those
Who demonstrate mortality.
If you die quickly from the dose
You'll be a "prompt fatality".
Many more may slowly go
If they're particularly hardy.
But who on earth would want to know
That their fatality was tardy?

But don't we need that nuclear power
To keep our factories on line?
Isn't every kilowatt hour
Required to keep our life-style fine?
Alternatives are rather dirty.
Coal pollutes and oil hides thirty
Thousand feet beneath the ground
With not much left there to be found.

There is one place that we could turn
For energy. No need to burn
Uranium in such great haste,
Producing piles of deadly waste
That no one knows just how to treat.
The **sun** could give us power and heat!

Those gentlemen in Washington
Who spend their time now sloshing tons
Of cash into uranium fission
Seem to think that it's their mission
To say that solar never can
Contribute to our power supply.
But do you know that in Japan
They see things with a different eye,
Investing millions to ensure
That when you think it's time for your
Own roof to carry solar tiles
They'll be ahead of us by miles!

Fund Raiser

In many countries, television's
Financed by the government,
Who then make programming decisions
With political intent.
Their output may all tend to bore
And lack a lot in verve and dash,
But luckily they can ignore
The need to hustle lots of cash.

Other countries find solutions
Somewhat like the BBC's.
They fund that splendid institution
By exacting license fees.
Vans patrol the streets and alleys
Armed with sensitive antennae,
Sniffing out unlicensed tellies,
Fining folk a pretty penny.
Covert viewers, when they're caught,
Before the magistrate are brought.
He sentences with no remission
Those who watch without permission.

Here in the U. S. of A.
We do things in a different way.
No one asks you for a permit
If you watch Big Bird or Kermit;
For Brideshead Revisited
No license fee's requisited:
But if you have the inclination
To a volunt'ry donation,
And send money flowing in you
Help this station to continue.

If you withhold your contribution,
There will be no retribution.
They won't give you nasty jolts
By sending twenty thousand volts
Along your television cable
To blast your set right off its table.
They won't fuel your Freudian fears
And amputate your rabbit ears
Because you just won't pay their price—
The people here are far too nice.

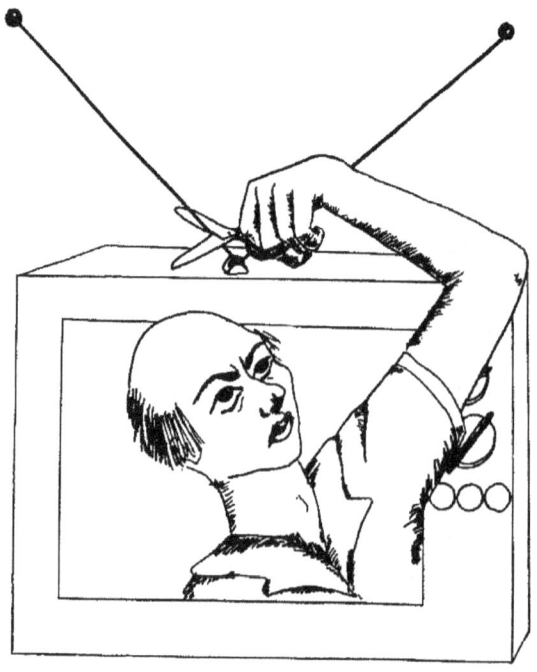

But what if no one heard their call?
This station would go to the wall
And then there'd be a punishment
For us to face — it's banishment
To stations where advertisements
Intrude. And though no hurt is meant,
It's hard to watch a serious play
That's interrupted just to say
That aerosols and laxatives
And miracle new wax that gives
A luster to your Naugahyde
Should elbow Shakespeare quite aside.

So though we do not need a license,
What we do need is a high sense
Of responsibility
To see that quality TV,
Which faces hardships, as we know,
Can, with our help, both thrive and grow.

Environmental Artifacts

The Environmental Protection Agency — the EPA — hired a public relations consultant whose task was to coach officials on how to deal with the press.

We have a little problem now—
Officials who just don't know how
To phrase descriptions of their work
In such a way that there won't lurk
Too great an element of truth.
You see, we think it quite uncouth
To let the public know our goals,
Which are to weaken all controls
Upon pollution of our air
And water, and to not impair
Those firms who gave to our campaign.
We'd like to see them once again
Each give a hefty contribution
Of their profits from pollution.
        It is in really awful taste
        To speak of "dumping toxic waste"—
        A poorly chosen phrase, by which meant
        Simply "chemical enrichment".
Another term one should avoid
Is "acid rain". I get annoyed
And find it hard to stay quite placid
When they say our rain is acid.
Such a phrase seems to recall
Harsh cloudbursts of pure vitriol.
Why should we suffer this abuse?
There's acid in pure lemon juice!
A nicer name that now I think all
Right is "gentle lemon sprinkle".
        Also we should all deride
        Description of formaldehyde
        As "causative of nasal cancer".
        There I think the simple answer
        Is that anyone exposed
        To risk of cancer of the nose
        Is much less likely then to die
        From any other malady;
        He is less likely then to go
        From heart attack, or vertigo.

Now we've stopped all real enforcement
Of the law, this has, of course, meant
That the sky is dark with grime;
So now is the ideal time
To say it is our predilection
To provide sunburn protection.

Daily we fire personnel,
Though that's not what we want to tell
The public. When to them we're speaking
It's efficiency we're seeking.
More work done by fewer people—
That's the way that we will keep all
Critics from their harsh complaining
Till there's no one here remaining.

When at last we've won the day,
And there is no more EPA
There is one problem that bodes ill—
How can we then continue still
To pull the wool across your eyes
With no one left to tell you lies?

Sorry— You've Been Troubled

The Rand Corporation completed a national study in which it listed 84 suburbs that it considered to be "troubled". The criteria they used as indications of being "troubled" included lack of growth in housing, low average income, and a high proportion of elderly or minorities.

We're such a fine suburb in Randbury Heights;
Living anywhere else would appall us.
Our houses are new, and we're nearly all whites,
So that "troubled" they never will call us.

We're mostly quite young — a condition we keep
With an interesting piece of logistics.
When people get old then we put them to sleep,
And that's great for our vital statistics.

Our average income grows steadily higher;
Such hard work will always bear fruit.
If any executive dares to retire
Then we give him a newspaper route.

To build lots of houses we've got what it takes,
Although space doesn't leave us much leeway.
We've built on the parks and the playgrounds and lakes,
And we're starting to build on the freeway.

These new housing starts put a burden on parts
Of the system — our sewers grow worse.
If we don't take our showers at pre-assigned hours
The plumbing goes into reverse.

Our minority couple just gave birth to twins,
So our black population then doubled.
We've asked them to get out of town for their sins;
You see, we don't want to be "troubled".

∞

Sperm Wail II

The Repository for Germinal Choice, which allowed women to have children fathered by Nobel Prize winners, announced the birth of its first product in April 1982.

> To some, experiments genetic
> Border on the unaesthetic.
> Others, who are more ambitious
> For their offspring, say they wish us
> To desist from petty quibbling
> At the way their children's siblings
> Have been duly fertilized
> By products of the Nobel Prized.

Thus moral qualms did not deter
One woman, who announced that her
Position was that she desired
That her next infant should be sired
By one whose brain had such a size
That he had won a Nobel Prize,
And her next bout of pregnancy
Would give a reason to rejoice,
If it came from a trip to the
Reposit'ry for Germinal Choice.

Well, she pursued her stated aim.
'Twas nine months later that it came
To pass that she announced the birth
Of one whose intellectual worth
Might be expected to be rated
Very highly elevated.

But what made many eyebrows rise
And took the world quite by surprise
Was news that this ambitious mother
Previously had led another
Altogether different life
From that of the ideal wife.
A charge of mail fraud had arisen,
Sending her to federal prison.

This knowledge puts a different face
Upon the hope the human race
Could be improved by using clinics
Trained in up-to-date eugenics.
Do we really want to breed
A race that's destined to succeed
By masterminding serious crime?
And is it really now the time
To cross a genius with a crook?
That hybrid could rewrite the book
On burglary and larceny
And murder, while at arson he
Could calculate ingenious ways
To set the very seas ablaze.
We'd feel much safer in our homes
If those who give out chromosomes
Would work to see that by next summer
Criminals would be much dumber.

Perhaps I'm being too dramatic,
Judging this inheritance.
Genetic laws are quite erratic,
Leading us a merry dance,
So one should not be too emphatic
That this little babe won't grow
Despite its origin synthetic
Into someone good but slow.

∞

City Ordnance

The town of Kennesaw, Georgia passed a law requiring all heads of households to own and maintain a firearm and ammunition. There was a $50 fine for violations.

They've passed a law in my home town;
It says that, when the chips are down
We must look after Number One.
For that we all must own a gun.

They've told us why we need this law:
Though nature's red in tooth and claw
We humans have got nature beaten;
We must eat or else be eaten.

When a burglar comes to visit
I won't stop to wonder, is it
Counter to his civil rights
To line him up between my sights.

Bang! Bang! That's how I'll greet that bleeder!
Oh? It was the meter reader?
Still, the principle's the same:
If you get shot, then you're to blame.

I've bought myself a forty-five
To help my neighbors stay alive.
My wife, who thought this too dramatic,
Has a little automatic.

And the children, bless their hearts,
Are taking up the martial arts.
To graduate from second grade
They have to toss a hand grenade.

They pull the pin, then count to five,
Then throw it, so they stay alive.
Poor little Jane finds that a chore
As she can't yet count up to four.

Because we're all so law-abiding
Some of us are now deciding
That a pistol's rather small
And hardly is a gun at all.
To stay within the law, we figure,
Calls for something slightly bigger.
Granny Brown says now it's her
Desire to buy a howitzer,
But then her house is very small.
Maybe she'll keep it in the hall.
If only it were three feet shorter!
Perhaps she'll settle for a mortar.

Uncle Fred thinks he will get
A brand-new French-made Exocet,
Although he'll have to modify
The guidance scheme, so it will fly
Much lower, then make its attack
Upon some passing Pontiac.

Last year at Christmas, I recall,
Some carol singers came to call.
They sang in such a festive mood
We asked them in, and gave them food.
Two barrels of fine cheese we'd made;
We gave them drink and then we bade
Them once again their plates replenish.
A whole cheese barrel did they finish!

This year, if they come singing carols,
I think they well might get both barrels.

Stone Deaf

A naval commander was unsuccessful in trying to track a foreign submarine. He blamed his failure on the bad hearing of his young sonar operators, and said they had been listening to too much loud rock music.

Part I

When Ulysses his greatest journey made
A host of perils in his path were laid.
A one-eyed giant sought to eat his crew;
He saved his men, and then in parting slew
The hungry Cyclops lest it should pursue
His weary band, who thereupon withdrew,
And soon set sail upon their journey home.
But as their vessel cleaved the salty foam
They faced the greatest danger of them all—
The Sirens — maidens beautiful and tall,
Who with seductive voice gave out pure song,
Bewitching mortal men, who then would long
For nothing save to hasten to that place
From whence those voices issued, there to face
But shipwreck on sharp rocks which lay uncharted
'Neath the waves. They'd perish brokenhearted
That those watery depths, which none had gauged,
Would drown them with their longings unassuaged.

Now Ulysses, who knew a trick or two,
At once determined what he had to do,
And stuffed his crewmen's ears quite full of wax
To render them immune from heart attacks.
He had his crew then bind him to the mast,
And when with double knots he was made fast
He bade his men sail swiftly as they dared
For home, their hearing totally impaired.

Part II

How strange it is that in these modern days
Defensive actions have reversed their phase:
A sailor's ears now need to be acute
So when a foe torpedoes starts to shoot
And sonar echoes bounce in Neptune's realm
The captain can be told to turn the helm,
And underwater sound waves' weak diffraction
Urges him to take evasive action.
Woe betide the ship whose sonar crew
Have penchant for Led Zeppelin, or The Who,
And from exposure in their local disco
Have dulled ears, and put their ship at risk,
Omitting, in their taste for decibels,
To think for whom will sound some future knells.

Thus do we see that deafness, once a boon,
Can now impede not just a Siren's tune
But also can that sound attenuate
That saves a seaman from a watery fate.
Patrolling submarines, all fully charged
With nuclear missiles, mightily enlarged,
Ensuring each could fry some distant city,
Prowl the ocean depths. It is a pity
That their crew, now edgy with the fears
That rock-and-roll has blanketed their ears,
Grow trigger-happy, fearing they'll be sunk
Before their task is done, all thanks to punk.
They strain to hear the sonar's distant sound.
Will they have time to fire before they're drowned?
If not, their country's forces face defeat,
And so each side adds warships to its fleet.
The politicians fail to heed the call
That says we need more missiles not at all
To turn the world into a fiery ball.
Are they, perhaps, the deafest ones of all?

∞

Pac-Mate

A manufacturer of home video equipment took legal action against a company that was producing sex-themed games for use on their consoles.

To uphold the good names of our video games
We are taking those villains to court;
For we really can't handle the taint and the scandal
Of sexual videosport.

I ask you, would you play a game that was blue?
Such a thing I would not waste a glance on;
And that's why we'll sue, 'cos we're nothing to do
With that Pac-Man who can't keep his pants on.

It's really outrageous to see Space Invaders
Make war in this porno production.
They don't use the tactic of weapons galactic
But conquer by simple seduction.

We do think it's wrong to produce Donkey Kong
In a form that's packed full of perversion.
That little man's tough, but he has work enough
Without giving him extra exertion.

We've become wealthy with games that are healthy,
And this year our profits quintupled.
We'd curl up with shame if we'd sold you a game
That showed Pac-Man and Ms. Pac-Man coupled.

So don't let your daughters and sons feed in quarters
To such a lubricious machine,
Just to see some Venusians perform their ablutions
Then do something not very clean.

But between you and me, what we hate most to see
Is something that's really a shocker—
The youth who exclaims that all videogames
Are a bore, and goes out and plays soccer.

∞

Behind the Highball

A man tried to sue a Baltimore bar because he became so drunk that he fell off the bar stool and broke his leg.

When I get in my car, and drive out to a bar,
I'm in search of some calm relaxation.
I'm really upset you allowed me to get
To a state of deep intoxication.

You must be a punk to have let me get drunk
When martinis my fancy had tickled.
You really should not serve me shot after shot
When you see that I'm thoroughly pickled.

Your job as a barman's to keep me from harm and
Slow down your supply of Manhattan.
I felt such a fool as I slid from the stool
Which I'd very unsteadily sat on.

Whenever I feel a strong urge for tequila
Or call for a big glass of bourbon,
Then if I'm cross-eyed, it's for you to decide
That my appetite you should be curbin'.

We know, you and I, that a man can get high
On a couple of six-packs of Coors;
But also we know that one gets very low
On one's back on your sidewalks and floors.

It's my inclination to seek out temptation,
And that's always been what my bent is.
Your duty's to be like a father to me;
You're my barman *in loco parentis*.

∞

Bones of Contention

Francis Brown, a geologist, and Noel Boaz, an anthropologist, cast doubt on the theory that "Lucy", a fossil found at Hadar in Ethiopia by Donald Johanson, was man's oldest hominid ancestor.

When Donald Johanson had first laid his hands on
The fossil he craved with such hunger,
He said "It appears she's aged four million years,
Though she may be a tiny bit younger."

With the bones from Hadar, in the footsteps of Darwin,
He redrew man's family tree.
With no further excuse he then christened her "Lucy",
And called in the press and TV.

But Noel T. Boaz then turned up his noaz.
Had Don taken leave of his senses?
The reason his nostrils were flaring was *Austral-*
-opithecus, called *Afarensis*,
Had lain in those canyons with several companions
(For fossils that isn't indecent)
A time, he'd report, a round million years shorter,
So Lucy must be much more recent.

Then Francis H. Brown had avowed with a frown
That Don's errors in dating were drastic;
"If he's so uncouth as to so stretch the truth
Then her name should have been Loose Elastic."
For an active volcano quite near where she'd lain
Overlaid her with ashes and stuff,
And it came as a shock that this volcanic rock
Was quite young. Said Johanson, "That's tuff."

That man, I aver, shall remain controversial
Despite all the fuss it's got him in.
That's what you expect if advice you neglect
And continue to date older women.

Bones of Less Contention
(a 2019 sequel to *Bones of Contention*)

*The discovery of Lucy in the Afar region of Ethiopia led to her species being named **afarensis**. A more primitive species, named **anamensis**, was thought to be the one from which **afarensis** had evolved, and so they would not have both lived at the same time. However, in 2016 a team led by Yohannes Haile-Selassie discovered an almost-complete **anamensis** cranium. This skull has now been determined to be younger than the oldest bones from Lucy's species. This suggests that the two species co-existed in the same Afar region. Like most startling discoveries, this one has its doubters.*

When Ali Bereino gazed at the terrain
Overlooking his fine herd of goats,
He feared that hyenas might invade the scene, as
They're known for their thirst for goat's throats.

His eyebrows he furrowed, then hastily burrowed
To make a safe den for his herd,
And 'twas then that he found, lying there in the ground,
Something formerly deeply interred.

'Twas a bone full of teeth, which had lain underneath
An abundant amount of manure,
So he seized it and ran to that very wise man
Who could say what that bone was, for sure.
Thus it was that Yohannes, for that's who that man is,
First learned of that wonderful fossil.
He went to that spot at a very fast trot,
For this find could be something colossal.

And when he arrived, where the herd of goats thrived,
He saw something just where they were grazing—
A rock that seemed dull there, was really a skull. Dare
One hope for a find so amazing?

He seized both the pieces, removed the goat feces,
And carefully placed them together.
They fit like a glove! And so, heavens above,
There could now be no doubt as to whether
Their previous owner, the bona fide donor,
Was really just one single creature.
The jaw he'd attached showed the skull was well matched,
In every significant feature,
To a previously known set of pieces of bone
Of a species now named *anamensis*,
Who'd lived, so they thought, with a feeling quite fraught,
Before Lucy, the famed *afarensis*.

The puzzle, you see, was the family tree
Of dear Lucy went back a long way.
Her ancient forebears 3.9 million years
Ago lived in their primitive way.

The new find was dated, Yohannes then stated,
An age 3.8 million years,
So this *anamensis* and some *afarensis*
Could've met and said "Hi!", it appears.

The previous thinking on this was unblinking—
The one had evolved from the other.
So how could it chime then, that at the same time
Both could live and p'rhaps meet one another?

Some critics felt pained, and one even complained
Saying this was just "one bridge too far".
But let's mute this insistence to doubt coexistence,
We know those bones came from Afar.

Vulnerable

At the height of the Cold War, the Reagan administration proposed a 17% increase in the military budget, but did not propose any new taxes to pay for this expansion.

The people who labor to see that our nation
Keeps up a strong milit'ry posture
Have lately expressed their extreme consternation.
That's bad, for its likely to cost your
Next hoped-for improvement in standard of living—
The Pentagon spends on a great scale.
It likes to encourage some generous giving,
And not just by having a bake sale.

Their shopping list now is as long as your arm,
For our nuclear strength needs much nourishing.
There's Cruise and MX, and, one hears with alarm,
There's a missile whose name sounds like "Perishing".

"Our present defenses are really quite weak"
Is the viewpoint they'd all like recorded.
And so we should give ev'ry dollar they seek?
That's incompetence richly rewarded!

We read in the news there's a missile called Cruise,
Which the Pentagon feels we can count on.
It reaches its target, not missing by far, getting
Fixes on each nearby mountain.
There is just one snag that may cause it to flag,
Just one failing that must be deplored;
It may get confused, for it's planned to be used
In a region that's flat as a board.
Northern Russia's vast steppes are not known for their hills,
Though that's data the Pentagon lacks,
But we think that this weapon could make lots of kills
If we aimed at the Adirondacks.

There's another new missile — it's called the MX—
Which may one day be pressed in to service :
But that would be bad, for its greatest effects
Would be simply to make Russians nervous.
Under Soviet attacks what the MX still lacks
Is a silo that it can stay fresh in.
The Russians say hence it's no use for defense,
So it's clear that we're planning aggression.

They're also quite scared now our plans have been bared
To locate our new Pershing II missile.
It's not that they find our intentions unkind
To equip it with substances fissile.
The thing that's alarming them's not how we're arming
It, putting plutonium in it.
It's rather our orders that Soviet borders
Be reached in well under six minutes.

That launch-pad in Germany won't let them defer many
Seconds their retaliation—
No time to run checks that there isn't a hex
In their radar-controlled computation.
Those Russians, one morning, might just "launch on warning",
Unleashing their nuclear terror.
It would be a pity to see ev'ry city
Destroyed by a programming error.

We've watched while our stockpile of weapons has grown;
What has shrunk is each one's credibility.
One does get the feeling all logic has flown
Out the window of vulnerability.

Cabbies Curbed

A new code of conduct for New York City taxi drivers prohibited them from "using physical force against a passenger".

Whenever you find yourself in the Big Apple
And look for some good transportation,
Just call for a taxi, and then you can scrap all
Your worry, your fear and frustration;

For now City Hall has just written a code
To forbid use of physical force,
So you'll never be slapped by those kings of the road—
That's unless you don't tip them, of course.

Those colorful fellows who drive city cabs
In the boroughs of Bronx and Manhattan
Have got to shape up, for the mayor's keeping tabs
On the number of people they've sat on.

Now if you take a cab, and request to go north,
And the cabbie starts heading due south,
Some gentle complaints you can now utter forth
Without fearing a punch in the mouth.

If he charges just double the authorized fare
And ignores what it says on the meter,
Thus causing some lady a protest to air,
From now on he's less likely to beat her.

But if he should throw this poor soul to the floor
Using language you're sure would appall her,
Lambasting her head with a thick two-by-four,
Ask him, "Don't you have anything smaller?"

∽

Thorns

The individual who delights
All those he meets upon the way
And brightens ev'ry neighbor's day
With cheery words that seem to say
That nature's full of happy sights—
The birds that sing, the flowers so bright,
So many things to drive the gray
Depressing clouds quite far away—
That man who turns the blackest night
To sunshine, with his friendly way
Of helping overcome one's fright
With thoughts of happiness and light,
That man, who never would incite
A colleague into an affray,
Just sometimes from exhaustion may
Become a little rough, and might
Show willingness to get in fights,
And people then could of him say,
"That giant has but feet of clay."
Though shock we'd feel at this relapse
His former kindness would perhaps
Remind us he's a decent chap,
So we would say, with little scorn,
"There is no rose without a thorn."

As on life's path a person goes
The milk of human kindness flows
Not everywhere, and I propose
It's also true that, heaven knows,
There's many a thorn without a rose!

Give Till It Hurts.

The Internal Revenue Service decided that the season in which people file their income tax returns was a good time to suggest that taxpayers might like to increase their payment with a charitable gift to the US government.

If you've the good luck to be fully employed—
A condition that not ev'ryone has enjoyed—
Then you know that you'll soon have to file a return
For the tax on the cash you were able to earn.

If you've labored all year on the factory floor
Just to keep on repelling the wolf from the door
Now's the time to be sure you don't squander your pay
Till you've done all the sums on your 1040A.

If you've dabbled in stocks and have traded in shares
You should watch out for shocks that may give you grey hairs.
Your accountant will give you his final report; he
May not have good news to put on your 1040.

But when you've completed this onerous task
And are giving the Feds every penny they ask,
And you'd like to sit down and relax with a drink,
For your duty is done, you complacently think,
Now the envelope's there with your tax return in it,
What more could they ask of you? Just wait a minute!

For now Uncle Sam has a novel proposal
For any spare money that's at your disposal:
Among the instructions for filing your taxes
There is to be found a suggestion that waxes
Most eloquently on the need some folk show
To be generous givers of more than they owe.
The instructions are there, if you take up their offers,
For mailing donations to Uncle Sam's coffers.

To this heart-felt appeal we should all be responsive
And take out our checkbooks and pens and at once give
A dollar or two, or some traveler's checks,
For the Pentagon needs it to buy the MX.
And don't give the excuse that you gave at the office. It
Won't help reduce our big federal deficit.

Also, you know that it really won't hurt you
To let it be seen you're a person of virtue,
For if you were called on to leave this world early,
And traveled straight up to those gates large and pearly,
And asked of St. Peter if you could go in,
And he looked up your name in a big book marked "Sin"
And he found that you'd led a most scurrilous life,
That you'd maltreated orphans and beaten your wife,
That you'd spread around town an unsocial disease,
And had failed to support a prompt nuclear freeze,
You could say to him "Pete, please admit me to Heaven, you
Know I've been kind to the Internal Revenue."

Asking For It

In 1982 the US Congress had passed an amendment to forbid the government from sending money to the right-wing Nicaraguan rebel groups known as "the Contras". The Iran-Contra scandal involved the discovery that the Reagan administration was secretly seeking other sources of funds. Secretary of State George Schultz or one of his aides was reported to have asked the Sultan of Brunei for money to send to the Contras.

Good morning, dear Sultan, George Schultz is my name,
And I'm here to make you a proposal:
We'd like you to give us, and here's why I came,
Any money that's at your disposal.

The reason we need it is easy to state—
There are Contras whose needs are quite pressing.
They're very nice people, I'm proud to relate;
Won't you give us some cash and your blessing?

They need to buy bullets and guns and grenades
And a lot of incendiary rockets;
It would help them along if you'd give them some aid
In their humanitarian projects.

We had hoped that Iran would come up with some green,
But their plight sets my heart quite a-bleeding.
They've spent all their cash blowing up our marines,
And so they can't afford what we're needing.

Don't think it undignified when Uncle Sam
Comes to Brunei with tin cup in hand.
It's congress's fault we got into this jam.
Tens and twenties? Yes, that would be grand!
To help things along,
Let me leave with a song:

    Once I built a railroad to the South
    To give the Contras more time.
    Congress said I couldn't — that's the truth.
    Sultan, can you spare a dime?

∞

Eppur si muove — And Yet, It Moves!

More than 350 years after the Inquisition had sentenced Galileo Galilei to life imprisonment for the heresy of suggesting that the Earth travels around the Sun, Pope John Paul II finally conceded that the Roman Catholic Church had erred.

Old Galileo wouldn't stay
Obedient to the Church,
But pinned his hopes on telescopes
And scientific search:
He said the sun could never run
A course around the Earth.
At first we tried these truths to hide
With scornfulness and mirth,
But he persisted with these twisted
Thoughts, and then in June
He tried to say, his stubborn way,
That Jupiter had moons!

To make things worse, the universe
(He claimed for all his worth
This utter rot) was clearly not
Now centered on the Earth!
These foolish schemes, these idle dreams
At length he saw were dumb.
He changed his mind lest we should wind
The screws down on his thumbs.
But we were fools to use such tools
To break that man's defiance.
We've learned the rack is not, alack,
An instrument of science.

It was absurd; we really erred
With poor old Galilei.
Now it's plain that our campaign
Was not an *opus dei*.

We do admit we were a bit
Off base with our conclusions;
But now we've found a law so sound
It won't permit confusion.

The human soul, it is our goal
To show without exception,
Must enter in the body in
The moment of conception.

That blastocyst, we must insist,
Could sin, and be forgiven;
That single cell could go to hell
If it should die unshriven.

This view, of course, we will enforce;
Our doctrine we can't soften;
But we won't get involved in threats—
At least, not very often.

Teacher's Aid

A National Commission had criticized the US educational system. It recommended tougher standards, longer school days, more homework, and better pay and preparation for teachers. The only response of the Federal Government was to continue to try and introduce prayer into the public-school curriculum.

There's been a report whose conclusion, in short,
Is that children are really not learning;
They haven't a clue how to count in base two,
As all difficult work they are spurning.

They're only in class for a very few hours
Of each day that their school is in session,
And those are not spent raising ten to large powers
Or with tough geometric progressions.

Performance in spelling is dropping quite fast,
And their English is simply appalling.
Now homework's become just a thing of the past,
Since most kids find TV more enthralling.

The present curriculum lets them ignore
Subjects rigorous or unforgiving,
And smiles on the student who studies folklore
Or takes courses in "bachelor living".

But let's not despair, for some help is at hand:
Have you heard what our President's saying?
He won't fund more teachers, but I understand
That his plan is to get students praying.

To halt education's continued decline
There's an utterly simple solution:
No need for more cash, everything will be fine—
Just amend the U.S. constitution.

If students can pray at the start of the day
They can get by with underpaid teachers.
But be not afraid, for we are sending aid—
Twenty rabbis, ten nuns, and twelve preachers.

Those teachers do really eat well on their pay
(Don't the students keep giving them apples?)
So that's why all federal funds from today
Will be used for constructing school chapels.

So please don't complain if your schooling is poor
And don't say the decision's unfair.
If you want Uncle Sam to help you off the floor
Then I'm sorry, you haven't a prayer.

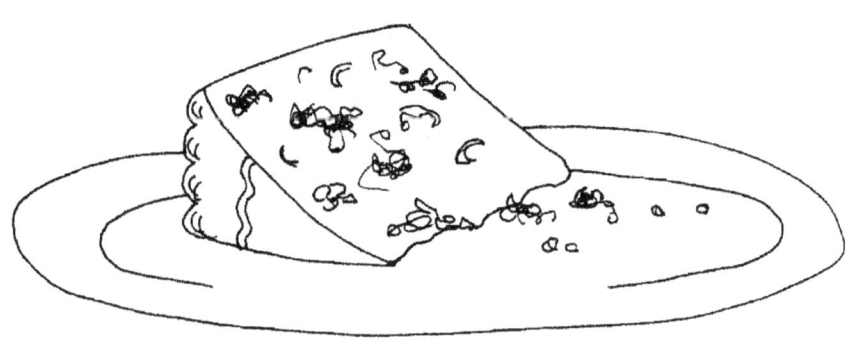

Let Them Eat Cake

Another component of the Iran-Contra scandal involved an attempt to raise funds by secretly selling arms to Iran, which was then engaged in a war with Iraq. As the US had declared Iran to be a State Sponsor of Terrorism, this move was difficult to justify. The cover story was that, within the Iranian government, there were "moderate elements" with which to negotiate. National Security Advisor Robert McFarlane was sent to Tehran with gifts of a chocolate cake and a bible signed personally by Ronald Reagan. This surely deserved a poem.

McFarlane and North took a trip to Iran
And, according to sources reliable,
To help them succeed in their ambitious plan
Carried gifts of a cake and a bible.

The President wanted the hostages freed
And he hoped that some arms he could barter,
So he said to McFarlane "Go see what they need.
Say I'm nicer than President Carter.

"And tell them I'm terribly anxious to deal.
Be sincere so it won't sound a fake tale;
And give them a fruit cake with cherries and peel.
Pick one up at the Pentagon bake sale.

"They want F-15's? We've got dozens to spare;
That they're terrorists just has no relevance.
To forgive them their trespasses is only fair;
I'm in love with their moderate elements.

"In their war with Iraq, tell them just how we know
That they need a new armaments shipper.
Say we're right on their side, and our slogan is 'Go
Ayatollah', win one for the Gipper."

∽

Free Cheese

Generous subsidies to the dairy industry had resulted in a glut of dairy products, forcing the government to buy up huge quantities in order to maintain prices. In 1982 the Reagan administration had the brilliant idea of cutting the budget for food stamps for the poor, while simultaneously distributing a quarter of a million pounds of surplus cheese to those in need.

We know times are hard, and there's much unemployment,
On this everybody agrees.
So we're helping the poor: for their dining enjoyment
We're giving them all some free cheese.

Thus to one poor old man we dished out Parmesan;
Another received Double Gloucester.
One old lady got a big chunk of Ricotta,
And not one red cent did it cost her.

If anyone's starving there's always a chance
We can help him to fill up his belly.
He may have to settle for old Liederkrantz
And then either be hungry or smelly.

Perhaps you'll run into some unlucky feller
Who fears that this winter he'll freeze.
Just tell him we'll send him a nice Mozzarella
If only he'll smile and say "Cheese".

I do sometimes think, as I'm handing out Brie
Or distributing ripe Provolone,
That as a response to a poor person's plea,
It's inadequate, cheap, and quite phony.

One cheese that we never distribute is Swiss,
Though its virtues our doctor extols.
Like the theories that brought unemployment like this,
It's just totally riddled with holes.

∞

The Pied Piper of Cleveland

The final poem in this book is a little different from those it follows. Unconstrained by the demand for brevity imposed by any TV producer, it took the time to expand fully on an attempt to bring Robert Browning's classic "The Pied Piper of Hamelin" into the late 20th century. In Browning's poem, written in 1842 but based on a fourteenth-century legend, a mysterious Piper offers to rid the town of its plague of rats in return for a thousand guilders. After he does so, however, the mayor of the town refuses to pay up, with the consequence that the enraged piper then bewitches the children of the townsfolk into following him into a mountain cavern that then closes upon them forever.

The theme that rich people are not always to be relied on to pay their bills promptly is still timely. My 1983 modification of the Robert Browning story carried a sub-theme that video games are an attractant that can distance children from parents. This idea has had surprising longevity; the only difference that nearly forty years have brought is that the video arcade has been replaced by the iPhone and the iPad.

Canto I

The City of Cleveland's a curious place;
Located on Lake Erie's southerly shore,
It had grown in the days when they transported ore
To the steel mills that formed its industrial core,
And brought wealth in their sooty and grimy embrace.
But then in the wake of the second world war
Heavy industry found that its outlook was poor,
So the city put on a new corporate face,
And from products to services turned its endeavors,
Aware that its sturdy old factories never
Again could compete with what came from Japan.
And so was developed a tactical plan
To restore to the city its corporate health
By creating new sources of copious wealth.
While others are dealing in dirty commodities
Clevelanders now will remark just how odd it is
Not to have realized ages before
That the way to accumulate assets galore
Is most certainly not to import iron ore
But confine one's attentions to money itself.

So when a young man seeks a fortune to earn he's
Most likely to enter a firm of attorneys
For there he can manage to wheel and to deal
Without ever messing with iron or steel.
The way to make money to leave to your kids
Is by specializing in takeover bids,
Or in filing long briefs as a friend of the courts,
And accusing opposing attorneys of torts.

The city's good fortunes now gathered new strength.
With the help of these lawyers, whose ideas were nifty,
Until trouble came, as it had to at length,
In a couple of years, 'twas around 1950,
Which threatened to put a swift end to this caper;
The plague that engulfed their endeavor was — paper!
It covered the desks and it filled up the drawers,
And then it spilled over the wide office floors,
And threatened to burst through the buildings' thick doors.
Invoices, ledgers, and thick bills of lading,
Permits to authorize multiple trading,
Through mountains of memos each person was wading:
Efficiency gradually started degrading,
With hopes for prosperity rapidly fading.

The city was now in a terrible stew;
There was nobody there who could see what to do
That could possibly offer a promise to quell huge
Incursions of paper now forming a deluge.
The mayor's flushed countenance showed desperation
As, faced by the chairman of each corporation,
He struggled to stem their immense consternation
That came with the paper-induced inundation.
The chairmen, whose visages showed their dejection,
Avowed the campaign for the mayor's re-election
Was sure to experience massive defection;
On their contributions he should not be countin'
Unless he could topple their papery mountain.

Canto II

    Then the mayor's secretary
    Came and whispered in his ear
    That if for help he'd really care he
    Need not any longer fear:
    A message from the strangest man
    Now offered a mysterious plan.
    "That message — is it writ on paper?
    Can't I even here escape a
    Rendezvous with my demise,
    Those floods of officework supplies?"
    His secretary calmed his fears,
    And said the message would be spoken.
    Then the mayor dried his tears
    And looked a little less heartbroken;
    "Send him in, we'll hear his scheming
    Though I fear he may be dreaming
    If he thinks that he has planned a
    Way to stop all memoranda."

Into the room came the strangest of figures,
A curious smile adorning his lips.
His eyes were deep set and were scarcely much bigger
Or glowed much more brightly than silicon chips.
Around his stooped shoulders he carried a cape
That was woven entirely from magnetic tape,
And his large droopy hat put his eyebrows at risk,
For it seemed to be made from a big floppy disk.
Its crown bore a symbol that, plain to the eye, owed
Its luminous power to a light-giving diode.
The tag on his suitcase allowed one to say
That his previous stop had been in San Jose.
He advanced to the table and pulled from his briefcase
An item he swore would diminish their grief;
"Base your hopes on the speck that I hold in my fist — a
Replacement for paper — a tiny transistor.
Let nobody here my opinion dispute. A
Resource I provide, which is called a computer,
Will rapidly banish your cares and your troubles
By writing its words on some magnetic bubbles,
Or, if you should look for great speed in its functions,
Will do its computing on Josephson junctions.

Your problems with paper will soon be forgotten
If you will resolve to acquire what there's not an
Iota of doubt is the trend of the future—
The hardware and software with which you'll compute your
Past balances due and accounts that need billing;
Your profits will rise in a way that's most thrilling.
My price is quite modest I'm sure you'll agree
For I do not demand an exorbitant fee:
My reward if approved by your fiscal inspectors
Is merely a seat on your boards of directors."

The company chairmen, broad smiles on their faces,
Then smothered the stranger with hugs and embraces.
"Our Savior," they cried, "We accept your kind offers;
What's more you shall find that our corporate coffers
Will swiftly yield up, like the whale yielding Jonah,
Some truly magnificent seasonal bonus,
And added to this, just to lighten your cares,
Will be generous options to purchase our shares."
Then the trace of a smile could be seen in the eyes
Of the stranger, who answered these rapturous cries
By producing a green glowing video display,
On the screen of which flashed just two letters — "OK".

> Then, without a moment's pause
> The stranger swept across the floor.
> Unheeding of the loud applause
> With which the chairmen urged his cause
> He opened wide the oaken door
> And left as swiftly as he'd come.
> The mayor looked around for some
> Reminder of the stranger's call.
> At first he could see none at all
> But then a glint of sunlight shone
> In through the door from which he'd gone
> And put into the mayor's head
> The thought there was some silken thread
> A giant spider might have spun,
> Reflecting now the golden sun.
> Its path he followed with his eye
> To see its termination lie
> Right in the cathode ray display
> That quietly on his table lay
> Still uttering its calm "OK".

But now this gleaming, glassy thread
Began to pulse a ruby red
As throbbing streams of information
Borne by laser modulation
Rushed onto the mayor's table
Through this fiber optic cable.
Soon the video display
Bore messages that rushed to say
That interest rates were in decline,
Steam's low in boiler number nine!
That income tax collection slumps
And where were hidden toxic dumps,
That parking tickets overdue
Were now excessive; time to sue
The company whose paving work
Was full of potholes! Fire that turkey
Of a sewage plant director!
Don't continue to neglect a
Real need for renovation
Of the downtown subway station!
Swiftly, without hesitation
Flowed this stream of information.

Canto III

Before very long a complete transformation
Occurred as the city's chief problems were solved.
Ev'ry office received its own video station;
Like magic the mountains of paper dissolved.
There were smiles on the faces of chairmen and mayor
As they lost all remembrance of erstwhile despair.
Ev'ry company now had a place in the sun,
And decided prosperity really was fun,
And immediately split all their stock, 2 for 1.
And to mark this success then the mayor did his part; he
Announced he was throwing a fabulous party.
A twenty-course dinner was catered that fall
In the city's magnificent banqueting hall.
All the chairmen replied to the mayor's warm call
For a toast to the city, and God bless us all!
Ev'ry person there present then drank with abandon,
So nobody noticed the sound of a hand on
The latch of the door as the stranger returned,
His objective to claim the reward that he'd earned.
So he cleared his throat loudly to draw their attention,
Then smiled and politely announced his intention
To take up his seats on their boards of directors.
The chairmen all frowned, and could not recollect a
Reward being promised. They pursed their lips tightly,
Till one of their number said he didn't quite see
The need for advancement at such a fast pace.
Would the stranger not rather accept with good grace
Some more modest position? They might find a place
In the warehouse, and then if he learned how to toady and
Grovel they might make him building custodian.

> Not to be bested
> The mayor then suggested
> The stranger's request be rejected.
> His cute little caper
> Had rid them of paper—
> What's gone cannot be resurrected!

The stranger's face tightened, was this what he'd earned?
And he looked round the room with displeasure.
"It seems there's a lesson," he said, "to be learned,
Which I'll teach you in very good measure!
You'll find that my read-only memory banks
Can be programmed in quite a new fashion;
And people who give me inadequate thanks
See how quickly I settle their hash." In
A moment the stranger had swept through the door,
And the mayor breathed a sigh of relief.
"Well, I don't think that fellow will trouble us more.
Since he's not been to law school he won't know our lore
And will file inadmissible briefs."

The chairmen resumed their relaxed conversations
And quickly forgot the unwelcome intrusion,
Until the director of one corporation,
Who let his eyes wander toward the location
Of one of the mayor's new video stations,
Then leapt to his feet in a state of confusion,
For gone were the latest commodity figures,
Or details of how each year's profits grew bigger,

> For there in their place
> Was an image of space
> In which rockets flew courses
> Past alien forces
> And shot at them all with great vigor.

Canto IV

    A sudden silence fell upon the hall—
    A silence broken only by the sound
    Of electronic chirps and bleeps as all
    The rockets shot invaders to the ground.

Each chairman pondered slowly what this meant
While scarlet spaceships battled for their lives
Until each one, all ammunition spent
Fell lifeless from the sky, whereon survives
Alone the legend on the screen that reads
"Game Over". Silence then returns, complete—
A silence absolute, which slowly breeds
Uneasiness that even on the street
No children's voices longer can be heard.

Then finally, each man to action spurred
By fear his offspring may have come to harm
Leaps to the window, out of which to see
With apprehension, not quite yet alarm,
Across the road, where there had formerly
Been but a plain brick wall, its latticed face
Unbroken by a window or a door,
Now, off'ring to its neon-lit embrace,
Pulsating from its ceiling to its floor,
An archway labeled "Video Arcade".

To this seductive aperture converged
The children, on each eager face displayed
The joyous will to find themselves submerged
Deep in a world where one is never bored
Repelling an invading alien horde
Or dodging flaming barrels thrown from high
By some gorilla's electronic hand,
Or guiding airplanes through a purple sky
To bring them past all obstacles to land.

Then when this gate had welcomed in that throng
Of youngsters jostling, trying to be first
To test their hand and eye, and see how long
Their youthful quickness would resist the worst
That integrated circuits could set free,
The portal slowly shrank and disappeared,
Restoring to the wall a symmetry
That made it, now from all obstruction cleared,
Invariant to translation of the eye
By one brick's length. 'Twas useless now to try
To fix one's gaze on where the door had been,
To will its reappearance, so that when
The arcade let its face once more be seen
The children's happy voices could again
Be heard. But such deliv'rance was not found.
The wall remained, each brick on mocking brick
Securely in its own location bound,
Deflecting ev'ry eye through some strange trick,
Deceiving with redundant information,
Dazzling ev'ry gaze until each head
Was forced to turn and face the realization
That some strong attractive force had led
The children to submit each to the urge
To cross the threshold, never to emerge.

Canto V — Epilogue

But that was all quite long ago.
It must be several years or so
Since Cleveland suffered in this way
The retribution that, some say,
Has changed the city's way of life.
No longer does one hear of deals
In which some politician's wife,
The passage of due time reveals,
Has purchased plots of city land
On which to place a doughnut stand,
Evicting previous tenants off it
Just to show a whacking profit.
Never can the city council
Surreptitiously be found still
Adding to their private wealth
And jeopardizing public health
By letting factories dispose
Of oily wastes that, heaven knows,
Not only do assault the nose
But may indeed cause dreadful woes.
One can today swim in the river
Without damaging one's liver
And still smell just like a rose.
Now honesty is everywhere;
There is no deal that is not square.
Corruption simply cannot flourish
In a climate that won't nourish
Anything that's underhand,
Or likely to arouse suspicion,
Lest one might misunderstand
That people of their own volition
Now eschew duplicity
In suburb and in inner city.

So, my friends, let us be sure
To take to heart this story's moral.
Make no deal unless it's your
Intention that your word will for all
Time remain your solemn bond.
If you have offered cash or stock
To someone, mind that you respond
When payment's due, lest such a shock
As visited those greedy men
Be given you. So once more, then,
No matter if you're under stress
That brings you to the brink of tears,
Remember — never, never mess
With electronic engineers.

About the Author

Philip Taylor has been writing funny poems since the 1980's, when his rhyming political commentaries became a hit on the weekly program "Signatures" on Cleveland's public television station WVIZ. All this humor had been thoroughly repressed in his day job as a Professor at Case Western Reserve University, in which his copious writing on topics like "A Quantum Approach to Condensed Matter Physics" provided zero opportunity for wisecracks and drollery. Although he has no fewer than six physics phenomena named after him, he shrugs off his fame in science with the modest exhortation "Ah, but you should read my poetry if you want a real laugh!" We should all take his advice.

∽

www.ingramcontent.com/pod-product-compliance
Lightning Source LLC
Chambersburg PA
CBHW081501070526
44586CB00019B/2452